THE DIR
MY BLOOD EARLY

Memories of Dirt Track Racing
In East Tennessee

By Scott Lasley

With grateful appreciation to:

My Lord and Savior Jesus Christ
My wife Brenda
My Mom and Dad, Betty and Jay Lasley, R.I.P.

Contents

The Dirt Got in My Blood Early

This is a story of my life, and dirt track racing cars and tracks, and the drivers who powered and drove the fastest machines.

Someone once said that when you get a taste of the dirt in your blood it never comes out. Well, if my blood was to be tested it would show red clay dirt, to the point where I would play in the dirt as a small child after a Saturday night trip to the local dirt track. I would take my hands and construct my own dirt track in the dirt. As the dust would fly I must have made a thousand tracks. Then I would take an old die cast-constructed car and roll it around in the dirt, sliding in the turn as I had seen so many great drivers do.

Wearing a pair of cut-off jeans, no t-shirt and being barefooted, dirty and sweaty, I must have run a zillion laps and won thousands of races. Then at school on Monday morning I recall taking a piece of notebook paper and drawing the cars I had watched run the past weekend, being careful to not let my teacher share my creative artwork.

Something about drinking a cold Coke covered with dirt dust, eating an old cold hamburger or a hard hotdog bun, the taste was so much better while watching the cars race, and dust wasn't an issue while eating the dirt-covered food. Most parents nowadays would have their child at the asthma or allergy center so fast it would make your head swim.

Sitting on the old bleachers, which were called grandstands, my Mom and Dad had friends that they sat with week after week, but me, I would sit down on the front row of seats being careful in some instances to watch out for splinters in my butt, and being sure not to sit on a row where the only person was a fat man or fat woman.

If you did sit on that empty row you had to keep one eye on the race and one eye on the fat person or persons sitting on the end, because when they got excited and jumped up because of a wreck or something, to my surprise I would be vaulted up like a carnival clown being shot out of a cannon.

Then, after the winners took the checkered flag, the gate under the flagman was flung open and all the people would rush to the infield to see and visit with each favorite driver. Once the gate flung open I was the first one in the pits to see as many drivers as I could before they would load the cars up and go to the pay window to collect the winning money they earned for that night of racing.

As the night grew longer the concession had a reduced price on the items they hadn't sold, so I ran to my parents, getting a quarter so I could purchase food items that had been reduced. What a way to have a dinner! Not much of a balanced diet, but who cared? I was there for the races, and since I was skinny I had no weight issue. I was in my comfort zone, if you call it fun to be sitting and watching the cars race and getting smacked in the arms, legs, and face with dirt ball marbles that were slung off by the cars going around the track. Most kids grew up playing Little League baseball or other sports, but my world was all about racing. Although I never drove a race car, I wonder how my life would have been if I had followed my heart and decided to drive.

My First Dirt Track; Broadway Speedway

Growing up in the early 1950s, I went to my first dirt track race at the old, now destroyed, Broadway Speedway in what is now Halls, just a few miles from the outskirts of Knoxville, Tennessee. The track was closed in the early 1960s and now is a stockyard. My first memory of the track is my mother carrying me on her hip because I had a broken foot, the result of being a three-year-old pulling a daredevil stunts, jumping off my aunt's back porch.

As a small child on a Saturday night back in the early Fifties I recall being at the dirt track as I saw the dust boil from the cars casting a shadow that almost blocked the light from the infield lights placed in and around the speedway. Down the track I remember such drivers as Wayne Fielden. (My dad grew up with him and told me there was a bounty on Wayne. The bounty was $100 back then and was for any driver who could beat Mr. Fielden and win the feature race.)

Many drivers, most of whom are now deceased include Kenny Metler, Hubert (Tootle) Estes who apparently had a heart attack while leaving the track at Volunteer Speedway in Bulls Gap, Tennessee, at age 52 after winning the feature race. Tootle and Kenny Metler was once barred from Georgia short tracks because of a winning streak of 29 races in a row, a feat no other dirt track driver in this area had ever come close to. Other drivers included Claude Lay, Claude Donovan, Paul Goose, Ed Harvey, Bobby Seymour, Bill Corum, Melvin Corum, Herman Collin, Kenny Sharp, and a very colorful driver named Breezy Waddell who later became a Flagman at various race tracks.

Skeeter Cars at Boyd Speedway

From there my racing memories go to the old Boyd Speedway in Chattanooga; riding in the automobile to the races with my dad and Wayne Fielden, as Hershel Alfrey the long-time mechanic from the Broadway Speedway would tow the green Number 2 car to the track. The cars were called "skeeters," which was a car body that was cut in half and reduced to a small size that had a wing on it. The skeeter cars raced at the old now Boyd Speedway along with such racers named the Alabama gang which consisted of Bobby Allison, Donnie Allison, and Red Farmer. These men got the title of the Alabama Gang because when the trio of drivers arrived at the track the local and other drivers would say, "Here comes that Alabama gang.

Other drivers there included Tootle Estes, G.C. Spencer, Coo-Coo Marlin (father of NASCAR racer Sterling Marlin), and brothers Harold and Freddie Fryer. The speeds and cars had become faster and the knowledge had increased and the cars would whiz around the speedway at speeds in excess of 100 miles per hour. Tragically, Freddie Fryer was racing when his drive shaft broke and came through the floorboard of his race car and he was killed while competing in a race.

Racing in Claxton with the Huffakers

My next racing memory comes from a little dirt track in Claxton, Tennessee. A track that was dirt and was located on Edgemoor Road. Back then it was between Oak Ridge and Knoxville. Now it is the home of the Tennessee Valley Authority Bull Run steam power plant. I remember going to the races with my parents and our next-door neighbors, Stanley (Fritz) Huffaker and his wife, Juanita, and their son, Gary Huffaker, who was related to a driver named Budd Rodgers who drove a purple Ford numbered 2 and called the "Purple Deuce."

Buddy was a young man who knew his way around a race track and won many feature races and was the driver that everyone knew they had to outrun. Buddy's mechanic was named Calvin Turner. Their race car stayed near Calvin's house on Shamrock Avenue, just down from St. Mary's Hospital in North Knoxville. As a young kid I was amazed in knowing a race car driver. Since Buddy was related to the Huffakers, I went to the garage where the Purple Deuce was stored with Gary Huffaker. I remember looking at the race car sitting still and the smell of the oil and motor smell and the odor the tires gave off. I remember looking and touching the race car and Gary letting me sit in the driver's seat. As a seven-year-old boy sitting in an actual race car, that was a highlight that all my friends at school would hear about.

Buddy and Calvin had a team that was unbeatable, as the trophies would attest. Such racers as Sherman Howell, M.C. Kerr, Herman Collins, Randal Byrd and a new young driver came on the scene. This young driver named H.E. Vinyard drove the Number 4 car and was up up-and-coming driver, but he couldn't outrun my idol, Buddy Rodgers.

A Race Car Right Next Door

The next memory I recall is our next-door neighbors, Gary Huffaker and his family, building a race car to compete on a track located in Newport, Tennessee, and to think I was living right next door to the actual owners of a real dirt track car! The car was bought and stripped of the front and rear fenders. My dad was a welder by trade, and they asked him to build the roll bars, roll cage, and front and rear bumpers for the car. I went with Gary Huffaker to the machine shop where the wheels were cut in half and welded to make the tires wider. I also remember the Huffakers taking the motor to an engine ship in Somerset, Kentucky, to have the race car's engine built to specs. The motor was delivered to Somerset and was returned several weeks later, fine-tuned and race ready. The engine was then installed into the body of the unpainted and unfinished race car. It was granted that my job consisted of holding the drop light, as the mechanics worked on the race car. I was paid no money but did get more than money could buy. After school, while the owners of the yellow and black trimmed Number 22 were at work I would rush home, do my homework and grab a bite to eat. After that I would be waiting at the basement door of the Huffakers and after the men came home and unlocked the door I ran to my drop light, turning it on and admiring the still sitting uncompleted race car.

I would hold the light and listen to the racing stories from the mechanics and onlookers. An occasional warning followed about me holding the list still, or "here, shine the light this direction," and if I wasn't careful the metal cover around the drop light would touch my arm or hand and burn me. After one good burn I was forced to keep my focus on the building of the car and a little less on the tales of who ran good at last week's races.

Week by week the race car was finished, and all it needed was a paint job. The paint was a bright yellow, trimmed around the windows with black and emblazoned with the number 22. Herman Goddard was chosen to drive the racer. Herman was a young driver who could drive the wheels off a race car, and he soon became my local hero. Herman's personal auto was a jet black, prettiest 1959 Chevy Impala, and it was always showroom ready. I admired the '59 black fins on the car more than any other street car I had ever seen.

Herman drove the race car many weekends at a track named Ashway Speedway in Jefferson City, Tennessee, owned by a farmer named Mr. Hillard. His son, Tommy, would run the track along with Mr. Hillard. The track was called "The Cow Pasture" because Mr. Hillard would turn cows in the track during the week and gather them up on Friday afternoon. Thus, you had to be careful where you stepped during the races if you were in the pit area, and because the lighting was so dim you could sometimes feel a cow patty under your feet after darkness fell.

Names I'll Always Remember

I remember such names as Cleve Jones, who drove a '38 Chevy numbered I-6; and another colorful driver named Windy York who drove a '38 Chevy with a Cadillac motor, white and numbered 87, with a Confederate flag attached to the passenger window roof. The faster Windy drove the more the flag would wave.

At one point Windy was in a race and it started raining. Well, Windy was a smart driver and knew the track was so slick that he would spin his race car out if he continued around the four-tenths mile track, so he began cutting through the first and second turns then cutting through the third and fourth turns, going to the edge of the fresh loose dirt, thus giving him more traction. Finally, the race was called because of rain delay, but old Windy was ahead of the game.

Another colorful driver was Roy Haun, who drove the number 30 blue Pure car with the Pure Oil decal painted on the side. Roy was a hard charger who won many races at the Cow Pasture. A lot of the drivers referred to Roy Haun's car as "The Dirty 30" because Roy and crew never washed the race car. Another was J.C. Lay who drove a '34 Ford with a Chevy engine.

Another was Pete Huffaker (no relation to my next-door neighbors). Pete would always dress in a maroon shirt and white jeans and his pit crew and sons would dress alike. Pete drove the number 44 car and was also a strong contender.

Another was Ralph (Duck) Moore, who was a Vestal native in Knoxville and raced a black '38 Dodge coupe with a big duck head cartoon character painted on the side. Duck was a powerful driver who seemed to enjoy a good fist fight at the race track as much as he enjoyed racing the car.

Another driver was Allen Love who drove and was a mechanic or parts manager for Beaty Chevrolet in Knoxville. Allen had a garage near us and sometimes we would go visit to see what secrets we could learn. One time I recall Allen telling the story about being outside the number 4 turn at the Cow Pasture, off over the bank. While using the bathroom he recalled a car flew out over the track and went over the men's head that wre using the bathroom.

I also recall a driver named Melvin Corum, along with his brother, Bill Corum, and their cousin Big Bill Corum. Melvin raced a '40 Ford sedan car number 1 with the back end cut off. Back in those days the sedans would cut the back end off at the back window. Big Bill Corum drive a gold-painted number 7 racer. I believe it was a '40 Ford coupe, and Little Bill Corum drive a pink '40 Ford numbered 21. The Corum boys were of the most powerful teams that ever raced the Cow Pasture, and one of the three would win on a regular basis.

Herman Collins was a full-time milk route operator and drove on weekends for the love of it. Herman drove a '40 Ford sedan and was also a strong contender.

Claude Donovan drove a race car that was painted refrigerator while and numbered 6. Later on in his career Claude was in a wreck on a track in Elizabethtown, Kentucky, and died from the injuries a few years later.

Buddy Rogers drove a black number 25 called the Black Widow with a figure of a black widow spider painted on the car. Another driver was Jack (Snake) Harper, along with Jack Phillips. Another driver was Pig Wilson

A motor inspector of the dirt racing was a barber named Archie Morris. Mr. Morris ran a barber shop at the north end of Central Avenue in Knoxville. I remember going with Gary Huffaker, my next door neighbor, to Archie's barber shop where

Archie could give one of the best flat top haircuts and tell all the racing stories of drivers and races he had been a part of. He knew flat-head motors inside out.

Purses and Protests

If a driver or team protested the winner, it would cost $25 to protest, or as the drivers would call it "tearing down." After a race it was not uncommon to see Archie Morris huddled over a flathead engine performing motor specification. If the car in question proved to be within the guidelines it was declared an official win. If the car that was protested was proven legal, the owner kept the "put up" money or the "tear down" money. If the winning car was found illegal then the win was taken away and given to the next finisher of the race, in addition to the winner's purse.

Speaking of purses, the winning driver and car owner had a set agreement on prize money or tow money. Tow money was money paid by the track to a team or driver that didn't maker or finish a race and was paid after each race. The drivers and owners had a set agreement on the money aspect of racing. The owner would collect 60 percent and the driver 40 percent of the week's earnings. A driver could win somewhere in the range of $40 to $75, depending if he won his heat race and fast car dash and feature. The races back then consisted of two heat races each of 15 laps, a fast car dash that was 15 laps, a consolation race for non-winners that was also 15 laps, and then a 50-lap feature race in which all drivers would compete. These races would be run on Saturday night and most drivers just raced in the regular Saturday series.

After that all the drivers moved to the then-Tennessee/Carolina Speedway, or as we called it the Newport Speedway, which was located at the fairgrounds in Cocke County, nestled in the foothills of English Mountain near the Smoky Mountain National Park. The track was a full half-mile dirt track that was the fastest track around the area. This was the big leagues of dirt track racing. On June 15, 1957, the race was won by Marvin

Panch who was a regular on the NASCAR circuit. He won the two-hundred lap main event. Another famous name was Glenn (Fireball) Roberts who won the race at Newport Speedway on October 7, 1956 and later was in a wreck at Charlotte Motor Speedway during a NASCAR race. He crashed and died from injuries from burns on July 2, 1964.

Another famous driver to race at Newport Speedway was L.D. Ottinger, a Newport Native. He went on to race in the NASCAR Grand National Division with a lot of driving success.

Don Collins drove a '40 Ford coupe, orange, number 92, with the back cut out at the back windshield. Another driver was named "Big Indian." He was full-blooded Indian. If you're seen the Jack Nicholson movie "One Flew over the Cuckoo's Nest," you may recall a character they called "Chief" in the movie. The race car driver named "Big Indian" looked exactly like the movie actor.

There was also a driver named Greasy Roberts, and a brother team based in Dandridge, Bill and Stew McMahan. Bill McMahan drove a red number 33 car and was a constant winner at the track. Another driver was named Ralph Moss. All the Drivers who raced at the tracks mentioned here were also regular drivers at Ashway Speedway.

Tragedy at Newport

As Mr. and Mrs. Huffaker would drive to the Newport Speedway, my parents would ride together while I would ride with the son, Gary Huffaker, towing the race car behind a 1957 Studebaker. Upon arrival at the race track I had to get out of the race car at the pit entrance and then go site with the adult women up in the stands while the men would all go to the pit road where the started to prepare the race car for the packing of the track. A water truck filled with spraying water would wet the track to keep dust down.

And then on August 19, 1961, as a 10-year-old kid, my racing world was shocked. After packing the track down it was time to go racing. Gary Huffaker was to start the first heat race in the family race car. When the field came around to take the green flag, something happened that changed many lives from that point forever. As Gary Huffaker was in the last row on the outside the start flag waved, and the car beside Gary lost control and ran into the outside of the pit grounds. Sliding into the infield, the out-of-control car knocked down a judges' scoring stand. As men on the stand were knocked to the ground, the car continued to slide out of control onto a group of men standing on the edge of the pits as the dust boiled. I remember seeing Mr. Huffaker get knocked down, and I recall Mr. Benny Price also getting struck. (Mr. Price was a neighbor who lived three houses down and was at the dirt track races for his first time ever. These are the type of neighbors that when it became Halloween time I would rush over next door and down to the third house at 4 p.m. to collect candy from him.) A third man named Mr. Huff from Newport was also struck by the car.

As the race was halted I remember rushing to the fence from the grandstand, climbing the fence, cutting my hands on the barbed wire, and then as the crowd stood in shock I recall seeing my father stand up dusting the red dirt off his clothes. I knew my dad was safe.

The Cocke County Rescue Squad loaded the men in ambulances, putting Mr. Huffaker and Mr. Price along with Mr. Huff into the Rescue Squad vehicle. Then my dad came into the stands to explain what had happened. Dad's shirt was torn and ripped in the back, but he didn't receive a scratch. At that point Mrs. Huffaker, my mom, my dad and I drove Mr. Huffaker's car to the hospital in downtown Newport, called Valentine-Schultz Clinic. I walked into the clinic and down the hall, I noticed a door cracked open and could see the men's tangled, crushed bodies lying in the floor. All three men were dead.

Mrs. Price was expecting a child. She stood in shock as the doctors informed the families their loved ones were dead. My next-door neighbor would never again say things like, "Gosh dang, Scott, hold the light still," as he had done in the past while building a race car. Gary had lost his best friend and his dad. That event changed our lives forever. Gary Huffaker would never race again; my dad wouldn't go to a race for years.

Returning to the Track; 411 Speedway

Several years passed after the terrible accident at Newport before my dad decided to go to the races again. When he did, we went to 411 Speedway, located off Chapman Highway, south of Knoxville, on Highway 411. The track, which was as the base of the Smoky Mountains in Seymour, Tennessee, was owned by Mr. Coy Floyd and featured Saturday night races. It was 1963, and I was 12 years old.

Being a rambunctious young boy, I would have footraces behind the grandstand with my friends, Ricky Collins and the Smith brothers, Jerry and Ronnie. Another foot racer was Rocky Estes, son of Tootle Estes, who was driving a race car in the car races. As we would run, our parents had no idea we were competing harder than the drivers on the track. As we would run from one end, behind the grandstands, we would see a security officer who would say, "You boys need to get in your seats and stop running back here."

We would say, "Thank you, sir," then race back to the other end of the grandstand. Upon arrival at the other end of the grandstand we would her a voice saying, "You boys need to go sit down and stop running." As a look of amazement ran all over our faces, we finally decided that the security guards were twin brothers. No way could the same security guard be at the other end of the grandstand waiting on us

The track now had a "B Class" division which we referred to as "jalopies." They were 1957 Fords that had a small motor and were less expensive to build and run. One driver who was a winner in the B Class was Monk White. Drivers named Otis Smiley and Tex Gibson, all of whom were good enough to drive with the older, experienced limited class drivers, chose to run in the B Class.

This was some of the best racing I can remember, as I would be ready by 3 p.m. to leave to go to the races, and it took was one holler from my dad saying, "Time to go to 411" and I was out the door, sitting in the back seat, with my fastest pair of tennis shoes, ready for the 45-minute ride to the track.

Bikes and Basketball

During that summer of 1963, I would ride my bike from our home near St. Mary's Hospital through the Lincoln Park neighborhood to a closed business located off Atlantic Avenue beheld Kelso Oil Company. There we built a bicycle race track out of the red dirt of a vacant service yard for an old out-of-business company that made concrete tile. This was in the area off of Broadway in North Knoxville, near Fulton High School, where I later graduated in 1969.

The Smith boys (Jerry, Ronnie, and Terry), Lewis Love Jr., and I were regulars at the bike track. The racing was fierce, with an occasional wreck that required soap and water and a Band-Aid® when we got home. I don't know which event, racing our bikes or going to the 411 Speedway, covered us with the most dirt.

Then I got interested in basketball in junior high school and my racing experiences slowed down, if not stalled. I became so involved with basketball that I didn't go to the races for a few years, but no amount of soap, water, and Band-Aids could get the racing dirt out of my blood. I missed racing and figured I could do basketball and still enjoy the competition of the engines roaring and the smell of the burnt motor oil that comes from the motor of a dirt track car.

Knoxville Raceway; No Dirt on the Hot Dogs

By that time (1965) my dad and mom were going to an asphalt race track named Knoxville Raceway, located on Highway 33 in Union County, north of Knoxville just beyond the Knox County line. At that track I recall the cars didn't sling dirt like the days of old. The cars didn't have the flexibility and couldn't slide through the turns like the cars on the dirt tracks, and besides, you and your food couldn't get covered with a thick layer of red clay dirt like I was used to from the earlier dirt tracks. But I decided, "What the heck, I'll watch the racing."

After a few weeks I saw drivers like H.E. Vinyard and Steve Smith, and Claude Lay was the flagman. Claude was an old racer from years past who had been in his share of racing accidents. I remember he had injuries to a leg from an accident, but he still loved racing and wanted to be a flagman because of his love of racing. He had a son named J.C. Lay who drove race cars and was a very good driver.

Atomic Speedway and the Great Ticket Caper

The years passed and a new track was built, Atomic Speedway in Roane County, named for its proximity to the "Atomic City" of Oak Ridge. Starting around 1973, my friend Dwayne Beeler and I would go to Atomic Speedway, which would soon be billed as the fastest three-eighths mile dirt track in the world.

Being a young man I didn't have much money, mostly because I would spend what little extra money I had trying to get my 1970 Pontiac GTO to continue running, buying car parts and tires. Dwayne and I decided we would beat the system. We went to Star Discount Sales on Central Avenue in Knoxville, where we could purchase a roll of tickets. They came in eight different colors and were just generic tickets for the admission gate at Atomic Speedway. We would put a ticket of each color in our shirt pocket and walk up to see what color the ticket window was selling that night. After we found the color that was being purchased by the regular paying customers, we would do a quick turnaround and dig in our shirt pockets for the matching color ticket, walk up and hand it to the ticket taker.

We mastered that art for three years until one evening at the start of the fourth season we walked up to the ticket window with the generic colored tickets in our shirt pockets to see what tickets they were selling. To our surprise, the tickets had changed. Dwayne and I looked at each other with that deer-in-the-headlights look, trying to figure out if the new ticket was now a reserved ticket that might have been added, or if they had got smart and caught us. With more than eight rolls of unused generic tickets, we now found our tickets obsolete and we had to purchase a ticket just like all the normal paying customers. Atomic Speedway had gotten modern and used a professional printer to print the admission tickets, so now we were regular paying customers as we sat and watched some of the best dirt track racing I had ever seen in my life.

Bob Martin was the track promoter and had leased the track and had atop field of quality drivers from all over the South as well as the regular local drivers competing on a weekly basis. One of the drivers was a redhead named Bill Elliott from Dawsonville, Georgia, who later went on to win a million dollars in NASCAR racing and also the NASCAR drivers championship. Some of the other drivers included:

- Doug Kenimer, who went on to be inducted into the Dirt Racing Hall of Fame and the Georgia Racing Hall of Fame;

- Mike Duvall;

- Jody Ridley;

- Ken Phillips;

- Steve Smith (runner-up to the dream winner at Eldora Speedway in Ohio with a purse of $1 million);

- H.E. Vinyard of Powell, Tennessee.

Another driver was Don Cox from Kentucky, who was one of the best up-and-coming drivers in the South, but his racing career was ended tragically by a fatal heart attack. Other drivers include Dale McDowell of Georgia, Freddie Smith of Louisiana (who now lives in Knoxville), Billy Palmer, Bill Ogle, Billy Ogle Jr., Lamar Wrinkler, Jack Trammell, Buddy Rodgers, Wayne Fielden, Sherman Howell, Zeke Buchanan, Shag Helton, Jimmy Monroe, Herman Goddard, Rusty Goddard, and Gary Hall.

Atomic Speedway was considered one of the best short dirt tracks in Tennessee and hosted many events with top prize money. Drivers who raced there include Dale McDowell, Earl Pearson Jr.,

Billy Moyers, Wendell Wallace, Anthony White, Jack Boggs and son Jackie Boggs, Ronnie Johnson, Mike Balzano, Chubb Frank, Jimmy Owens, Dwayne Hummell, Clint Smith, Randal Chupp, Rick Aukland, Skip Arp, Steve Francis, Bart Hartman, Wade Knowles, Darrell Lanagin, Bob Pierce, Jeff Purvis, and Rodney Combs.

The list goes on, but the most famous and winningest dirt track driver at an estimated earnings of more than $8 million is Scott Bloomquist from Mooresburg, Tennessee. Scott has won both the World 100 and the Dream 100 at the famous Eldora Speedway on several occasions. To this day Scott holds the record for fastest qualifier at Atomic Speedway, as well as racing at tracks in Alabama, Florida, and North and South Carolina. He also competes in Kentucky, Mississippi, and Georgia. Scott Bloomquist is both the most popular and the most unpopular driver in the world of outlaws late model dirt series.

I have fond memories of Atomic Speedway. The track was bought and torn down after the 2006 racing season, and a trucking company built a terminal on the property. Still, every time I drive down Interstate 40 at the Melton Hill exit, my mind wanders back to the many years of enjoyment that I and all the other dirt track fans shared. After three owners and 36 years of racing, Atomic Speedway is no longer roaring with engines on Saturday nights, with race cars sending dirt flooding the parking lot and blowing over Interstate 40.

Lo, the memories that track holds, and lo, the tales that track could tell if it could talk.

My Annual Pilgrimage to Eldora

Every December, my friend Steve Duncan and I, along with his son, Derick, make reservations for our race tickets and call and get motel reservations for the next September to attend the now-world-famous Eldora Speedway in Ohio, now owned by NASCAR race driver Tony Stewart. The event starts on the Wednesday night before the weekend of racing. As many as 200 cars with drivers from 18 states and Canada try to make the feature race of 24 cars.

Friday is filled with practice and qualifying times, then the Friday event ends with heat races where the drivers that qualify race to get a chance to get in the big event on Saturday night. The Friday night event can last until 3 a.m. Saturday.

Then on Saturday everyone gets up and goes to the track for more races to determine the final field. The final race is usually sold out, and finding a seat is as competitive as any track in NASCAR.

When the field is determined and it's time to race, all 24 cars line up doing a drive-by salute to the fans. Lined up four wide, the cars pass in a parade lap, waving a salute to the fans. As the green flag waves, butterflies jump in every fan's stomach. For some of the best racing outside of the NASCAR circuit, this little track nestled away in Ohio is in a class of its own.

Growing up watching racers and going to the many different tracks and eating the cold concession food has molded me into what I am now. I grew up in a simpler time. I didn't know what it was like to take a gun into school; instead, I took the memory of the past Saturday night's races. No drugs, no fighting in school, no video games, no wearing pants low on my hips, no jeans that dragged the ground. No cap tilted sideways or turned backwards on my head, no gold chains hanging and no cell phones ringing or text messages. No loud stereo car boom boxes, no spoke spinner wheels, no neon lights glowing under the frame of my automobile.

From playing with 97-cent toy match box cars as a young boy, my love for racing is as strong as ever. I now collect actual used race car doors and quarter panels from some of today's top dirt late model racers. My total sheet metal collection is approximately 25, in addition to my collection of factory made American Diecast Company cars of about 300 total. For more information, go to the Facebook site for Christian Diecast Collectors or Dirt Diecast Depot site.

Take Your Child to the Races; You'll Be Glad You Did

I feel racing has made me a person who respects speed limits and doesn't engage in road rage. My youth was a time when life was laid back. No stress and no pressure were placed on me. Today's children could learn from finding a role model who drives a race car such as those I grew up with. Not some professional basketball player who tests positive for drugs, or some baseball player who is so overrated that he doesn't have time to sign an autograph without charging for it. Walk up to Richard Petty and ask for an autograph and see how you are treated; then walk up to Derek Jeter and see if he will sign something without a charge.

The difference is, times have changed. I am thankful for the tracks, drivers, and mechanics I have known and the story tellers of racing memories. And for an entertaining Saturday night, take your family to a dirt track race. Create a memory for your child or children. When they get older they may call and say, "Dad, we're going to the dirt track races. Would you like to come with us?"

About the Author

Scott Lasley lives in Morristown, Tennessee, with his wife, Brenda. Born and raised in Knoxville, Tennessee, he graduated from Knoxville Fulton High School in 1969, attended Calvary College in Letcher, Kentucky, and played basketball at both schools.

He is retired from a career as a train conductor with Norfolk and Southern Railway. Scott was called as a young man to preach God's word, and he has answered that call through jail ministries, street corner preaching, and mission trips to Ukraine and the Philippines.

His hobbies include attending dirt track races and collecting a variety of related items, such as die cast dirt track cars, used doors from racing cars, dirt race car sheet metal, and other memorabilia.

Scott extends special thanks to John Schlatter, his friend and former Fulton High School basketball teammate, for his help in producing this book.

Made in the USA
Middletown, DE
16 April 2022

64205002R00018